Unwrapping a Book

USING NONFICTION TO TEACH WRITING IN THE PRIMARY CLASSROOM

Written by

Nicole Groeneweg

TWO HILLS MENNONITE SCHOOL

Ms. Arnold's ESL 4-6

Editor: Collene Dobelmann
Illustrator: Darcy Tom
Production: Carrie Rickmond
Designer: Moonhee Pak
Art Director: Tom Cochrane

Table of Contents

Introduction 3

Literature Resource 4

Getting Started 6
    Unwrap a Book 7

Features of Nonfiction Text 9
    Captions 10
    Time Lines 13
    Pronunciation Keys 16
    Labels 19
    Emphasized Vocabulary 22
    Photographs and Illustrations 25
    Glossaries 28
    Maps 31
    Fact Boxes 34

Writing Nonfiction Books 37
    Desert Book 38
    Alphabet Book 40
    Biography 43
    Field Guide to Animals 47
    How-to Book 50
    Photo Journal 52
    Time Line Book 55

Writing Periodicals 57
    Classroom Newspaper 58
    Sports for Kids Magazine 70

Special Forms of Nonfiction 72
    Brochures and Pamphlets 73
    Cards and Letters 75

Board Games and More 77
    Ideas Using Nonfiction 79
    Reading Response Log 80

Introduction

Nonfiction is an excellent source of read-aloud material for the classroom. Capturing and building on children's inherent wonder about the world around them is one of the many challenges teachers of the primary grades face. Through nonfiction texts, teachers can cultivate this interest while capitalizing on it to teach students to read, write, and learn concepts from an array of curricular areas. This resource will help you provide anchor experiences with expository text that will ensure your students become successful learners throughout their lives.

Unwrapping a Book introduces young children to the world of nonfiction by providing opportunities to read and write fact-based informational text. Children will be instructed in how to use the conventions of this genre and in turn use them in their own meaningful writing experiences. As a result, children will begin to read nonfiction with the critical eye of a writer, which increases comprehension.

Each activity has been successfully implemented with young children and features children's work. So, simply gather your students around you, and unwrap the mystery of nonfiction. You will surely produce readers and writers who are fascinated and brimming with questions and connections.

Literature Resource

Share with children these strong examples of nonfiction literature to give them a solid frame of reference for the features of nonfiction text.

	Captions	Time Lines	Pronunciation Keys	Labels	Emphasized Vocabulary	Photographs & Illustrations	Glossaries	Maps	Fact Boxes
ANIMALS									
Alaska's Three Bears by Shelley Gill						•		•	•
Amazing Sharks by Melvin Berger						•			
The Bird Alphabet Book by Jerry Pallotta						•			
The Butterfly Alphabet Book by Brian Cassie and Jerry Pallotta						•			
Chicks & Chickens by Gail Gibbons		•	•	•		•			
Desert Babies by Kathy Darling			•			•		•	•
Dinosaurs by Gail Gibbons			•			•			
The Emperor's Egg by Martin Jenkins					•	•		•	
From Egg to Chicken by Robin Nelson					•	•		•	
Gone Forever! An Alphabet of Extinct Animals by Sandra Markle and William Markle			•			•			
A Gull's Story: A Tale of Learning about Life, the Shore, and the ABCs by Frank Finale						•	•		
Horses by Gail Gibbons	•			•		•			
A House Spider's Life by John Himmelman					•	•			
Javelinas by Lola M. Schaefer						•			
Jellyfish by Elaine Landau						•	•		•
The Laziest: Amazing Facts about Lazy Animals by Mymi Doinet					•	•		•	•
Life Cycle of a Chicken by Angela Royston		•			•	•			
Look to the North: A Wolf Pup Diary by Jean Craighead George		•				•			
The Milk Makers by Gail Gibbons						•			
Prairie Dogs by Emery Bernhard	•					•	•	•	•
Sea Life by Katy Pike and Garda Turner						•			•
Seven Weeks on an Iceberg by Keith R. Potter	•			•	•	•		•	•
Stegosaurus and Other Plains Dinosaurs by Dougal Dixon	•		•			•	•		•
Supergiants! The Biggest Dinosaurs by Don Lessem		•				•			
The Ugliest: Amazing Facts about Ugly Animals by Mymi Doinet						•		•	
Why Do Horses Neigh? by Joan Holub			•	•		•			
PEOPLE									
Abe Lincoln: The Boy Who Loved Books by Kay Winters						•			
Claude Monet by John Malam						•	•		
George Washington Carver: The Peanut Wizard by Laura Driscoll					•	•			
I Can Be a Baseball Player by Carol Greene						•			
Martin's Big Words: The Life of Dr. Martin Luther King, Jr. by Doreen Rappaport		•			•	•			
Pirates: Robbers of the High Seas by Gail Gibbons						•		•	
The Pueblos by Alice K. Flanagan	•					•	•	•	
The Shawnee by Alice K. Flanagan	•		•			•	•	•	
A Weed Is a Flower: The Life of George Washington Carver by Aliki						•			

	Captions	Time Lines	Pronunciation Keys	Labels	Emphasized Vocabulary	Photographs & Illustrations	Glossaries	Maps	Fact Boxes
PLACES									
At the Post Office by Carol Greene						•			
Beacons of Light: Lighthouses by Gail Gibbons						•			
Cactus Hotel by Brenda Z. Guiberson		•				•			
Desert Giant: The World of the Saguaro Cactus by Barbara Bash			•	•		•			
The Desert Is My Mother by Pat Mora					•	•			
A Desert Scrapbook: Dawn to Dusk in the Sonoran Desert by Virginia Wright-Frierson	•		•	•		•			
Deserts by Gail Gibbons	•			•	•	•		•	
Dig, Wait, Listen: A Desert Toad's Tale by April Pulley Sayre					•	•			
PROCESSES									
Deadline! From News to Newspaper by Gail Gibbons		•			•	•			
Extra! Extra! The Who, What, Where, When and Why of Newspapers by Linda Granfield						•			
Farming by Gail Gibbons						•			
The Furry News: How to Make a Newspaper by Loreen Leedy	•					•	•		•
The Great Trash Bash by Loreen Leedy						•			
Here Comes the Mail by Gloria Skurzynski					•	•			
Lights! Camera! Action! How a Movie Is Made by Gail Gibbons					•	•			
Mail Carriers by Dee Ready				•		•	•		
The Post Office Book: Mail and How It Moves by Gail Gibbons						•		•	
Recycle! by Gail Gibbons	•			•	•	•			
Recycling by Rhonda Lucas Donald	•					•	•		•
Weather Forecasting by Gail Gibbons	•			•	•	•		•	•
What a Job! by Becky Gold						•			
Where Does the Garbage Go? by Paul Showers						•			
THINGS									
The Bicycle by Larry Hills	•	•	•	•	•	•			•
Bicycle Book by Gail Gibbons					•	•			
Bicycles by Lola M. Schaefer					•	•	•		
Cameras by Chris Oxlade					•	•	•		
Click! A Book about Cameras and Taking Pictures by Gail Gibbons					•	•			
Giant Sequoia Trees by Ginger Wadsworth			•			•	•	•	•
Going to My Gymnastics Class by Susan Kuklin						•			
Models by Helen Bliss					•	•			
The Moon Book by Gail Gibbons	•	•			•	•			
The Moon Seems to Change by Franklyn M. Branley	•	•		•		•			
Powwow by George Ancona						•			
The Quilting Bee by Gail Gibbons	•				•	•			
Rivers and Lakes by Simon Holland and Anna Lofthouse	•					•			
Soccer around the World by Dale E. Howard						•			
The Sun by Paulette Bourgeois	•	•		•	•	•	•		•
Tell Me, Tree by Gail Gibbons					•	•	•		
Wild West Days by David C. King					•	•			

Features of Nonfiction

The first section of this resource is designed to help children become familiar with features of nonfiction text, such as captions, labeling, and fact boxes. The lesson for each feature is broken down into three parts: Before the Text, Reading the Text, and Following the Text. The first step provides a method to introduce a particular skill, such as bringing in a real bicycle to label in order to introduce the concept of labeling. The second step offers a selection of books (to be read aloud) that include the nonfiction-text feature being taught. The third step gives children a meaningful way to practice the skill. The progression of each lesson ensures that children develop good habits while reading *and* writing nonfiction text. Children will collect their work, and put it in a folder labeled *Features of Nonfiction*.

Writing Nonfiction

When children are preparing to write their own nonfiction as described in the latter sections of this resource, encourage them to refer to their *Features of Nonfiction* folder. This will help children decide what information they want to include in their writing and how to present it.

Literature Resource

You may wish to extend a lesson on a particular text feature (e.g., labels or pronunciation keys). To find a list of trade books that contain specific text features, see the Literature Resource on pages 4 and 5. Each book is listed according to topic and the text features it utilizes.

It's important to note that many of the books suggested for use within this resource contain some fictional elements. However, their primary purpose is to convey information in different content areas, and these titles have great educational value.

Helpful Notes

Some of the writing activities in this resource call for blank hardcover books. If you cannot obtain the hardcover books, you may chose to make your own books from construction paper. Enlist the help of parent volunteers to preassemble the books for the class using binder rings or plastic binding combs.

Getting young children to analyze information, organize it, and write their own nonfiction can seem like a daunting task. Have children work in pairs so they can support one another. Also, use the reading selections suggested with each activity. They are age-appropriate and teach the desired skills.

Unwrap a Book

Introduce nonfiction literature to young children with this exciting technique. Be prepared for cheering when they see the wrapped big book on the book stand!

Reading Selections	Materials
Big books: ***Amazing Sharks*** by Melvin Berger (Newbridge Educational Publishing) ***The Milk Makers*** by Gail Gibbons (Aladdin)	» fadeless bulletin board paper » ribbon or bow » gift tag » tape

Building Children's Interest

Wrap the big book with fadeless bulletin board paper. Add a bow and gift tag to make it look like a gift from the author (e.g., perhaps the gift tag may read *To: Miss Groeneweg's Class, From: Gail Gibbons*). Let children hold and feel the wrapped package until someone guesses that the gift is a book. Ask the children what they think the book is about. With each response, ask them about their reasoning. If children do not notice it, point out the gift tag. A child familiar with the author may guess that it is a nonfiction book because it is "from" Gail Gibbons.

Keeping Children's Interest

Rip a tiny section of the paper, exposing a small portion of the cover. Ask children again what they think the book is about. A child may see part of a green pasture on the cover and conjecture that the setting is on a farm because it looks like a rural area. Then invite children to rip small sections. Discuss the cover as more of it becomes revealed. Children may notice black-and-white spots on the cover that look like part of a cow's body.

As more of the book is revealed, enthusiasm for the activity will grow, and richer discussion will evolve. Encourage children to use their knowledge of word chunks and blends when letters of the title become visible. Invite them to see if they can guess the title or subject of the book. A child may reveal the letters *M* and *i* and conclude that the book is probably about milking cows. Use this strategy to promote rich discussion, questions, and connections made by children throughout the process of unwrapping a nonfiction book. Read the book to the class. As you read, ask children to confirm or discount the predictions they made.

Features of Nonfiction Text

Give children opportunities to investigate nonfiction literature to provide a firm foundation for future comprehension of informational texts. This chapter provides teachers with clear and detailed lesson plans that introduce children to nonfiction features through direct exploration of text. Children will discover how authors use the following techniques to inform readers:

- » Captions
- » Time lines
- » Pronunciation keys
- » Labels
- » Emphasized vocabulary
- » Photographs & illustrations
- » Glossaries
- » Maps
- » Fact boxes

Give each child a folder labeled *Features of Nonfiction*. After every lesson in this section, have children place their completed assignment inside the folder. Ask children to keep their folder at their desk for easy reference when they are writing their own nonfiction.

Children will never read nonfiction text the same way again!

Captions

Authors of nonfiction often include important information in captions. Explain to children that captions are titles, short explanations, or descriptions that accompany an illustration or a photograph in nonfiction text. Children sometimes ignore this information, perceiving it as "extra," but getting children into the habit of reading captions leads to greater comprehension of nonfiction text. To teach this topic, choose a reading selection that best suits your students' interests.

Reading Selections	Materials
Horses by Gail Gibbons (Holiday House) ***Jellyfish*** by Elaine Landau (Children's Press) ***Rivers and Lakes*** by Simon Holland and Anna Lofthouse (DK Publishing) ***Stegosaurus and Other Plains Dinosaurs*** by Dougal Dixon (Picture Window Books)	» Clever Captions reproducible (page 12) » photographs or illustrations with captions » markers » sentence strips

Before the Text

Choose an illustration or photograph with a good caption to show the children. Cover the caption. Ask children what information they think the caption contains. Write a few of their ideas on sentence strips, and place them below the illustration. Then uncover the caption and discuss how the caption compares to the students' responses. Discuss how captions give important information that makes the illustration easier to understand.

Stegosaurus was a dinosaur that ate plants.

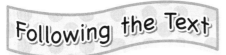

Read aloud your selection to the class. Point out the illustrations with captions as you read the book. Discuss how the text in the captions calls attention to specific and important information.

Following the Text

Distribute the Clever Captions reproducible (page 12) to children. If you are working with young children, you may wish to give one reproducible to each pair of children. Brainstorm a class definition for *caption*. Write the definition on the chalkboard, and have children write it in the space provided on the reproducible. Have children look at the pictures, and help them decide the importance of each image. For example, a child may say that grooming a horse is important because it helps keep the horse clean and healthy. Tell children to write their thoughts in the spaces provided. Then encourage them to draw a picture in the box and write an informative or helpful caption beside it. If children are working together on one reproducible, make a copy of their completed work so that each child has one. Ask children to place the completed sheets in their Features of Nonfiction folder.

A group of large animals is called a herd.

Name _____

Clever Captions

A caption is _____.

Write a caption below each picture.

_____   _____

_____   _____

Draw your own picture, and write a caption for it.

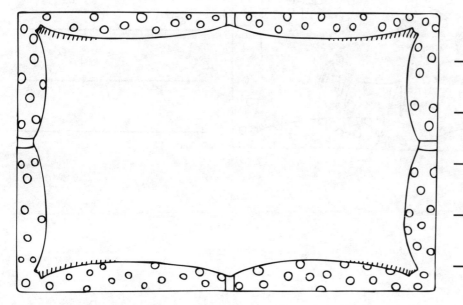

_____

_____

_____

_____

_____

Unwrapping a Book © 2006 Creative Teaching Press

Time Lines

Teach children how to read time lines so that they become focused, strategic, and independent readers. Time lines offer readers a point of reference when events occur over a period of time. Many nonfiction authors use time lines to share important information. To teach this topic, choose a reading selection that best suits your students' interests.

Reading Selections	Materials
Life Cycle of a Chicken by Angela Royston (Heinemann) *The Moon Book* by Gail Gibbons (Holiday House) *Supergiants! The Biggest Dinosaurs* by Don Lessem (Little, Brown and Company)	» My Milestones reproducible (page 15) » chart paper » markers

Before the Text

Create a chart with the months of the school year. Ask the children to think about important things that happened during each of these months. Chart their responses. Discuss changes that have occurred since the beginning of the school year. (If you use a portfolio system, this is an opportunity to have the children look at their own work and reflect on what they have learned each month since September).

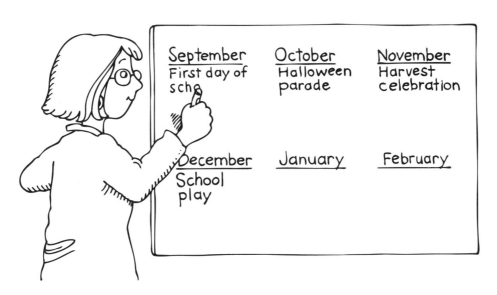

Reading the Text

Read your selection, emphasizing how things undergo change as time passes (e.g., the phases of the moon or the growth of a chick). Point out how the author chooses to show the information with time lines.

Following the Text

Distribute the My Milestones reproducible to children. Brainstorm a class definition for *time line*. Write the definition on the chalkboard, and have children write it in the space provided on their reproducible. Have children label the first column *September*, the second column *October*, and so on. If you are doing this activity early in the school year, you may wish to instruct children to write the name of the current month at the far right of the time line and help them name the months for the other corresponding spaces. Remind children to include the year. In the spaces below the months, have children write memorable events that occurred during that time. Ask children to place the completed sheets in the Features of Nonfiction folder.

2004   2005

Sept.	Oct.	Nov.	Dec.	Jan.
• School started • Learned about ocean	• Ocean festival • Studied forest	• Planted tulip bulbs in garden	• Made Cinderella carriage	• Studied desert

My Milestones

A time line is _____ _____ .

Make a time line of your school year. Include important things that happened to you this school year.

Pronunciation Keys

Nonfiction books often include pronunciation keys throughout the text. Express to children that beginning and experienced readers alike use pronunciation keys to aid them in pronouncing new vocabulary. Encourage children to use these keys to learn the number of syllables in a word and which syllable to stress. To teach this topic, choose a reading selection that best suits your students' interests.

Reading Selections	Materials
Dinosaurs by Gail Gibbons (Holiday House) **Giant Sequoia Trees** by Ginger Wadsworth (Lerner Publishing Group) **The Shawnee** by Alice K. Flanagan (Children's Press) **Why Do Horses Neigh?** by Joan Holub (Dial Books)	» Perfect Pronunciations reproducible (page 18) » markers » chart paper » dictionary

Before the Text

Write on a chart a word that is unknown to the children and difficult for them to pronounce (e.g., *monarch, stomachache, photograph*). Write the pronunciation key from a dictionary below the word, and cover it. Ask children to read the word. You may get some attempts—and avid readers may already know the word—but most children will "stumble" on the word. Reveal the pronunciation key, and guide them as they read it. The key should make the pronunciation of the word much easier. Ask children to read the word again. Have children use the key to determine the number of syllables. Encourage children to clap or snap as they say each syllable. Point out to children that the accented syllable is usually in boldfaced type.

Reading the Text

Read your selection to the class. Show how to use the pronunciation keys embedded in the text as you read. Include the children in interpreting the pronunciations of the unusual words. Ask children to note how the syllables are separated and how the accented syllables are indicated.

Following the Text

Have children work in pairs or small groups, and give each group a picture dictionary that includes pronunciation keys (*Scholastic First Dictionary* from Scholastic Reference is an excellent choice). Allow some time for exploration of the dictionary. Then encourage children to look for multisyllabic words that are unfamiliar to them. Distribute the Perfect Pronunciations reproducible (page 18). Have children choose one word from the dictionary and use the information to complete the reproducible. Ask children to place the Perfect Pronunciations sheet in their Features of Nonfiction folder.

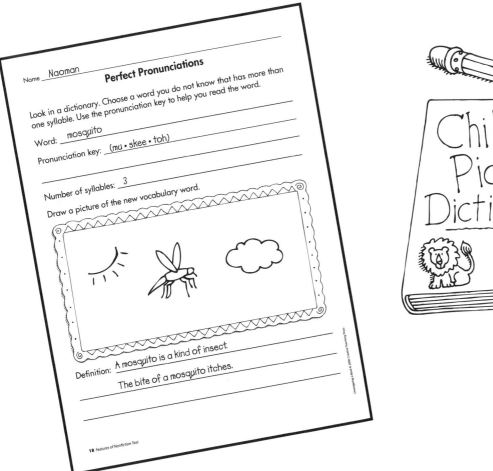

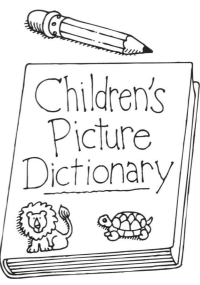

Perfect Pronunciations

Look in a dictionary. Choose a word you do not know that has more than one syllable. Use the pronunciation key to help you read the word.

Word: _____

Pronunciation key: _____

_____

Number of syllables: _____

Draw a picture of the new vocabulary word.

Definition: _____

_____

_____

Labels

Labeled illustrations are prevalent in nonfiction books. Young children can learn to recognize and use labels to maximize their learning of subject matter. Teach children to get into the habit of using labels to enhance their reading comprehension. Using a bicycle to demonstrate labeling is a helpful teaching method. Choose a book from the list below to expand on children's knowledge of bicycles and labeling.

Reading Selections	Materials
Bicycle Book by Gail Gibbons (Holiday House) **Bicycles** by Lola M. Schaefer (Bridgestone Books) **The Bicycle** by Larry Hills (Capstone Press)	» Learning with Labels reproducible (page 21) » bicycle » chart paper » sentence strips » markers » tape

Before the Text

Bring a real bicycle to school, and display it for the class. Ask the children to share what they know about bicycles. Write their responses on chart paper. Have children point out the parts of the bicycle they are familiar with. Help children use sentence strips and tape to label these parts on the bicycle. At first, this will probably be limited to the chain, seat, and a few others.

Reading the Text

Read aloud your selection. Point out to the class the labeled illustrations as you read, emphasizing names that are new or unfamiliar.

Following the Text

Ask children what new information they learned. Add their responses to the chart paper. Write vocabulary words from the book on sentence strips to make labels. Ask children to help label the bicycle. Invite them to tape the labels to the corresponding parts of the bicycle.

spoke	front axle	crank

Discuss how labels aid in learning new information. Define the term *labels* as a group. Students may suggest something similar to the following: *Labels show us the parts of an object.*

Distribute the Learning with Labels reproducible (page 21) to children. Have them draw a picture of their face and then label it. Ask children to place this labeled illustration in their Features of Nonfiction folder.

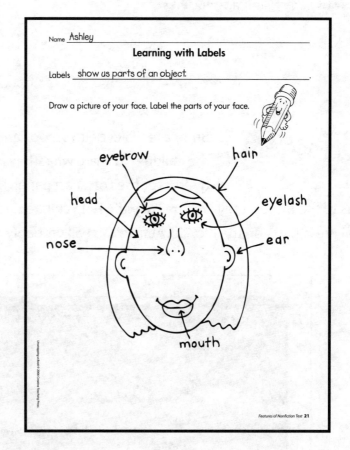

Name Ashley

Learning with Labels

Labels show us parts of an object.

Draw a picture of your face. Label the parts of your face.

eyebrow   hair   head   eyelash   nose   ear   mouth

Features of Nonfiction Text **21**

Name _____

Learning with Labels

Labels _____.

Draw a picture of your face. Label the parts of your face.

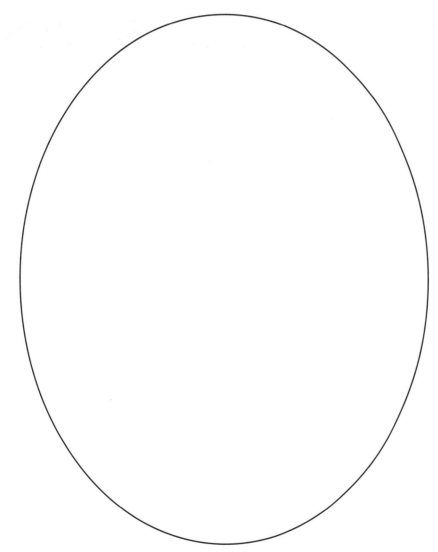

Emphasized Vocabulary

Nonfiction text is chock-full of new vocabulary. Often, authors emphasize these words and other key concepts to better attract the reader's attention. Various techniques, such as **bolding words**, *italicizing words*, <u>underlining words</u>, and enlarging words, are used to highlight these new terms. Recognizing these text features as important enables the reader to more fully understand the subject at hand. To teach this topic, choose a reading selection that best suits your students' interests.

Reading Selections	Materials
A House Spider's Life by John Himmelman (Scholastic)	» Vivid Vocabulary reproducible (page 24)
Seven Weeks on an Iceberg by Keith R. Potter (Chronicle Books)	» chart paper
Tell Me, Tree by Gail Gibbons (Little, Brown and Company)	» markers
	» highlighters

 Find a sentence from a nonfiction text that contains emphasized vocabulary. Copy this text onto chart paper, making sure to use the same technique the author did to accentuate the word. Show children the sentence. Ask them to note the word that looks different from the rest of the sentence. Discuss the reasons they think the text is different.

Reading the Text

Read aloud your selection, and point out to the class the emphasized vocabulary. Discuss the different ways the author grabs our attention (e.g., bolded text, italicized text, capitalized text, enlarged text, colored text). Some authors even use two or three techniques to accentuate these words. You may want to refer to this as *vivid vocabulary* or *cue words*.

Following the Text

Ask children to work in pairs, and hand each pair a different nonfiction book. Have the pairs leaf through their book to find examples of vivid vocabulary to share with the class. Brainstorm a class definition for *emphasized vocabulary*. Distribute the Vivid Vocabulary reproducible (page 24). Encourage children to choose an interesting example of vivid vocabulary, and have them copy the word on their reproducible. Tell children to copy it exactly the way it appears in the text (e.g., bolded, capitalized, colored). Ask children to place the completed sheets in their Features of Nonfiction folder.

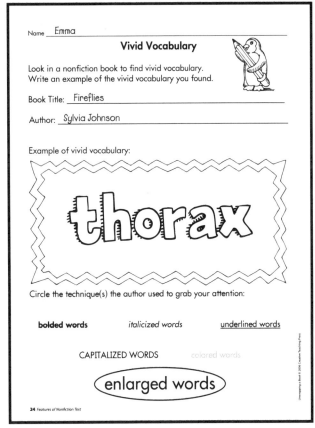

Name _Emma_

Vivid Vocabulary

Look in a nonfiction book to find vivid vocabulary. Write an example of the vivid vocabulary you found.

Book Title: _Fireflies_

Author: _Sylvia Johnson_

Example of vivid vocabulary:

thorax

Circle the technique(s) the author used to grab your attention:

bolded words   *italicized words*   underlined words

CAPITALIZED WORDS   colored words

(enlarged words)

24 *Features of Nonfiction Text*

Name _____

Vivid Vocabulary

Look in a nonfiction book to find vivid vocabulary.
Write an example of the vivid vocabulary you found.

Book Title: _____

Author: _____

Example of vivid vocabulary:

Circle the technique(s) the author used to grab your attention:

bolded words   *italicized words*   <u>underlined words</u>

CAPITALIZED WORDS   colored words

enlarged words

Photographs and Illustrations

A picture is worth a thousand words! Nonfiction authors use photographs and illustrations to impart information to readers. Teach children to scrutinize illustrations to further their comprehension. To teach this topic, choose a reading selection that best suits your students' interests.

Reading Selections	Materials
Beacons of Light: Lighthouses by Gail Gibbons (HarperCollins) **Desert Babies** by Kathy Darling (Walker & Company) **The Moon Seems to Change** by Franklyn M. Branley (HarperCollins) **Powwow** by George Ancona (Harcourt)	» Picture This reproducible (page 27) » pictures of animals and/or plants (1 per child) » markers » chart paper » scissors » glue

Before the Text

Distribute a picture of an animal or plant to pairs of children. Encourage them to look at details and discuss the picture. Then have children share with the class the information they gleaned from the picture. Write their observations on chart paper.

Reading the Text

Read your selection to the class. Point out the inset illustrations as you read. Choose a few of the illustrations to discuss in depth.

Following the Text

Distribute the Picture This reproducible (page 27) and the remaining pictures so that individual children have one of each. Encourage children to make an observation about their picture. Ask them questions such as *Does the animal or plant have any interesting features? Can you learn anything from the picture?* Have children use their pictures to complete the reproducible. Ask them to cut out and paste the picture in the space provided, and tell children to write a caption for it. Have them place the finished worksheet in their Features of Nonfiction folder.

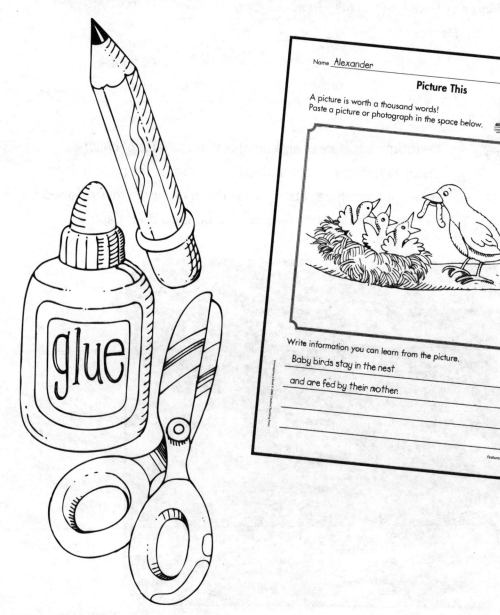

Name _Alexander_

Picture This

A picture is worth a thousand words!
Paste a picture or photograph in the space below.

Write information you can learn from the picture.
Baby birds stay in the nest
and are fed by their mother.

Features of Nonfiction Text **27**

Name _____

Picture This

A picture is worth a thousand words!
Paste a picture or photograph in the space below.

[picture space]

Write information you can learn from the picture.

_____

_____

_____

_____

Glossaries

Glossaries are included in many nonfiction books. New vocabulary is defined and placed in alphabetical order for easy reference. Children can deepen their understanding of text by using glossaries when they encounter unknown words. Teach children to refer to the glossary if they need help with a word. To teach this topic, choose a reading selection that best suits your students' interests.

Reading Selections	Materials
Farming by Gail Gibbons (Holiday House) *From Egg to Chicken* by Robin Nelson (Lerner Publishing Group) *The Sun* by Paulette Bourgeois (Kids Can Press)	» Wonderful Words reproducible (page 30) » sentence strips » tape » chart paper

Before the Text

Read aloud a paragraph from a nonfiction text that contains unusual vocabulary. Use a think-aloud technique to model for children how to use the glossary to determine the meaning of a new word. Tell children that nonfiction authors often use a glossary to define new vocabulary and that the glossary is placed at the end of the book.

Reading the Text

Read your selection to the class, and continue using a think-aloud technique to demonstrate using the glossary when you come across a word you think children may not understand. Involve them in helping you find the word so they can practice their knowledge of alphabetical order. Encourage children to conjecture why the words are listed in alphabetical order.

Following the Text

Write on sentence strips terms from your chosen reading selection, and tape the strips in random order on a chart. Ask the children to help arrange the terms as they would be in a glossary. Distribute other nonfiction texts that include glossaries to pairs of students. Allow them to share their observations with each other (e.g., some glossaries have illustrations, but most do not; words being defined are often boldfaced). Distribute the Wonderful Words reproducible (page 30). Have children use the observations they made to complete the reproducible. Children can complete the sheet in small groups or individually. Ask children to place the Wonderful Words reproducible in their Features of Nonfiction folder.

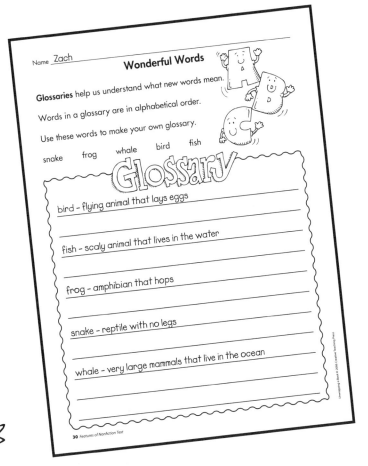

Name Zach

Wonderful Words

Glossaries help us understand what new words mean.

Words in a glossary are in alphabetical order.

Use these words to make your own glossary.

snake   frog   whale   bird   fish

Glossary

bird – flying animal that lays eggs

fish – scaly animal that lives in the water

frog – amphibian that hops

snake – reptile with no legs

whale – very large mammals that live in the ocean

30 Features of Nonfiction Text

Wonderful Words

Glossaries help us understand what new words mean.

Words in a glossary are in alphabetical order.

Use these words to make your own glossary.

snake   frog   whale   bird   fish

Glossary

_____

_____

_____

_____

_____

_____

_____

_____

_____

_____

Maps

Maps abound in nonfiction literature. Learning to read maps and other graphic aids enhances children's understanding of the subject and makes for a more independent reader. Teach children to interpret graphic aids by choosing the reading selection that best suits your students' interests.

Reading Selections	Materials
The Laziest: Amazing Facts about Lazy Animals by Mymi Doinet (Random House) ***Pirates: Robbers of the High Seas*** by Gail Gibbons (Little, Brown and Company) ***The Pueblos*** by Alice K. Flanagan (Children's Press) ***The Ugliest: Amazing Facts about Ugly Animals*** by Mymi Doinet (Random House)	» Meaningful Maps reproducible (page 33) » dot stickers » map or globe » map of your country or state

Before the Text

Have children place dot stickers on a map to locate where they were born. If you have an ethnically diverse class, you may want to use a globe to mark the countries the children's families descended from.

Reading the Text

Read your selection to the class, pointing out the maps as you read. Discuss why they are important to the text.

Following the Text

Review the maps pictured in the book. Working with children, find the locations on the classroom map. Discuss how nonfiction texts use maps to enhance important information. Display a map of your country, state, or province, and ask children to note its shape. Have children point out your city and the capital city. You may also wish to discuss elements unique to your area (e.g., geographical features, state flower, national bird, important crop).

Distribute the Meaningful Maps reproducible (page 33). Have children use the information to complete the reproducible. Encourage children who have moved from another state or country to use that information when completing the reproducible. Ask children to place the completed sheets in their Features of Nonfiction folder.

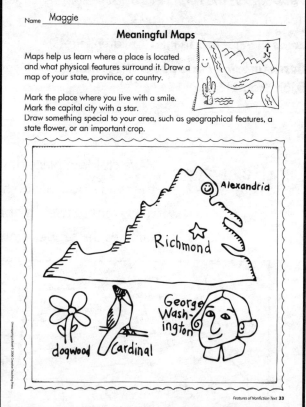

Name _____

Meaningful Maps

Maps help us learn where a place is located
and what physical features surround it. Draw a
map of your state, province, or country.

Mark the place where you live with a smile.
Mark the capital city with a star.
Draw something special to your area, such as geographical features, a
state flower, or an important crop.

Fact Boxes

Fact boxes appear when definitions or additional information are pertinent to illustrations or other texts. Young children often ignore these vital bits of information as they read nonfiction books. Learning to use these fact boxes leads to greater comprehension of nonfiction text. Familiarize children with fact boxes by choosing the reading selection that best suits your students' interests.

Reading Selections	Materials
Prairie Dogs by Emery Bernhard (Harcourt) **The Quilting Bee** by Gail Gibbons (HarperCollins) **Sea Life** by Katy Pike and Garda Turner (Chelsea Clubhouse) **Weather Forecasting** by Gail Gibbons (Aladdin)	» Fun Facts reproducible (page 36) » chart paper

Choose the book you will be sharing with the class. Write on a chart the facts the children already know about your subject of choice. Coach children into volunteering information by asking questions that pertain to your reading selection, such as: *What tools would a weather forecaster use? What kind of home do you think a prairie dog would make for itself? What is a baby whale called?*

Reading the Text

Read your selection to the class, pointing out the fact boxes as you read. Have children recognize that these facts are usually written in smaller or different fonts. Explain that this is because it adds interest to the page and isolates important information. Stress to children that it is important to notice each part of a page, not just the text in the main body paragraphs.

Following the Text

Discuss what was learned from the information contained in the fact boxes. Add that new information to your chart. Distribute the Fun Facts reproducible (page 36), and have children use their newly acquired knowledge to complete it. Ask children to place the completed sheets in their Features of Nonfiction folder.

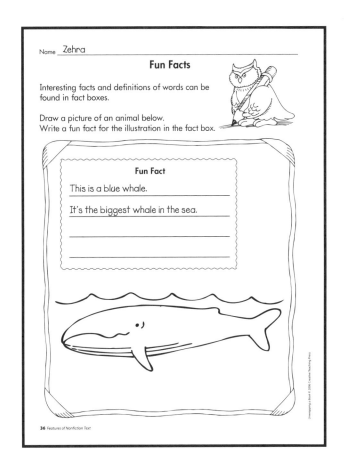

Name Zehra

Fun Facts

Interesting facts and definitions of words can be found in fact boxes.

Draw a picture of an animal below.
Write a fun fact for the illustration in the fact box.

Fun Fact

This is a blue whale.

It's the biggest whale in the sea.

36 Features of Nonfiction Text

Name _____

Fun Facts

Interesting facts and definitions of words can be found in fact boxes.

Draw a picture of an animal below.
Write a fun fact for the illustration in the fact box.

Fun Fact

_____

_____

_____

_____

Writing Nonfiction Books

Tell children that there are many different types of nonfiction and equally many ways to represent that information. For instance, an author may choose to write a book about deserts and break down the information by categories, revealing facts in an order that makes sense to him or her. Or an author may choose an ABC format, revealing information fact-by-fact according to letters in the alphabet. Biographies, field guides, how-to books, photo journals, and time lines are additional types of nonfiction this chapter explores. Encourage children to examine and practice all types of nonfiction writing by providing them with strong examples. Remind children to use their Features of Nonfiction folder if they need help organizing information.

Desert Book

Publish a nonfiction book about deserts in the classroom! Encourage children to use the nonfiction features they learned about in the previous chapter to write their own nonfiction books. Choose a nonfiction book about deserts to introduce the topic to the class, but have several books from the Reading Selections list on hand so children have multiple references. In addition to writing skills, children will learn about plant and animal life that live in a very dry region.

Reading Selections	Materials
Cactus Hotel by Brenda Z. Guiberson (Henry Holt and Company) ***Desert Giant: The World of the Saguaro Cactus*** by Barbara Bash (Sierra Club Books) ***The Desert Is My Mother*** by Pat Mora (Piñata Books) ***A Desert Scrapbook: Dawn to Dusk in the Sonoran Desert*** by Virginia Wright-Frierson (Aladdin) ***Deserts*** by Gail Gibbons (Holiday House) ***Dig, Wait, Listen: A Desert Toad's Tale*** by April Pulley Sayre (Greenwillow Books)	» chart paper » blank hardcover books (available through mail-order catalogs) » permanent markers and crayons » extra school photos » watercolor paints » paintbrushes » Features of Nonfiction folder

Before Writing

Read your selection(s) to the class. Then ask children to help you make a chart depicting the adaptations that desert plants and animals have made. Have children dictate to you unusual words and other interesting facts. Display this chart so children can use it as a resource when they write their book. Ask children to take out their Features of Nonfiction folder. Review with them the different types of text features. Discuss with children what information they would like to include in their books and what text features (e.g., illustrations, labels, fact boxes) will best emphasize important information.

Writing

Help children put their knowledge of nonfiction features to work. Focusing on and then utilizing these conventions ensures true understanding of the nature of nonfiction. Help children include text organizers such as a table of contents, an index, and a glossary. Ask children to use proper capitalization rules and alphabetical order when they are writing these text organizers.

Show children how to add page numbers after the informational component is written to ensure accuracy. Each book is carefully modeled after "real" books, so encourage children to add features such as a dedication page. Encourage children to use writers' terms frequently (e.g., *author, edit, publish*). This will instill in children a sense of importance and pride in their work.

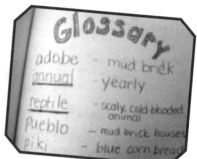

Publishing

Now children are ready to publish their work in blank hardcover books. Tell children their books must have a section devoted to honoring the author. Writing in third person about themselves is a difficult task for young children. Set aside some time to practice this skill with them. Ask children to include in their writing information they would like other people to know about them. For instance, a child may write what his or her hobbies are, or why he or she chose to write about a particular topic. When they are finished, invite children to glue an extra school photo to the page, and have them label the page *About the Author*.

To complete the process of publishing their own nonfiction book, ask children to make an appealing, yet informative, cover. Children love to use the technique of "crayon resist" to make the cover. First have children use crayons to draw the picture. Then ask them to paint over the picture with watercolor paints. Encourage children to include details like an ISBN code, a title on the spine, and excellence seals that give their book an authentic look. Challenge children to make these nonfiction books look as if they have been professionally published, and their creativity will soar. The children's books can be exhibited in the library and even given bar codes so they can be checked out!

Alphabet Book

It's as easy as ABC to teach a love for informational text! Children enjoy reading and writing facts in an ABC format. Have children write an ABC big book as a class. It's a simple way to reinforce the skill of reading nonfiction text for the purpose of learning information. The strategy can be used for *any* nonfiction book. Class big books are favorite reads for young learners because these books give children a sense of pride and ownership.

Reading Selections	Materials
The Bird Alphabet Book by Jerry Pallotta (Charlesbridge Publishing)	» abc book form reproducible (page 42)
Gone Forever! An Alphabet of Extinct Animals by Sandra Markle and William Markle (Atheneum Books)	» 11" x 17" (28 x 43 cm) paper
A Gull's Story: A Tale of Learning about Life, the Shore, and the ABCs by Frank Finale (Jersey Shore Publications)	» 12" x 18" (30.5 x 46 cm) construction paper
The Butterfly Alphabet Book by Brian Cassie and Jerry Pallotta (Charlesbridge Publishing)	» capital- and lowercase-letter cutouts
	» glue
	» hole punch
	» paper fasteners

Use a photocopier to enlarge the abc book form reproducible almost to the size of an 11" x 17" (28 x 43 cm) piece of paper. If you are unable to do this, use it as a guide to draw your own reproducible on 11" x 17" paper. Leave about 4 inches (10 cm) of blank space at the top of the page. Make 26 copies of the reproducible, and glue a capital- and a lowercase-letter cutout to each page. Then glue the pages onto the construction paper. Invite children to choose a book from the selections that piques their curiosity. Children can work in pairs or groups to read the text.

Writing

After children have read their book, give the letter pages to pairs or individual children. Ask children to choose interesting facts they learned from the text that correspond to their letter page, and have them write and draw those facts. Remind children to include the title of the book they read and the author's name at the top of the page. Encourage children to add interest to their page with carefully drawn illustrations and a border of letters matching the first letter of their subject. Remind them to sign the page they worked on!

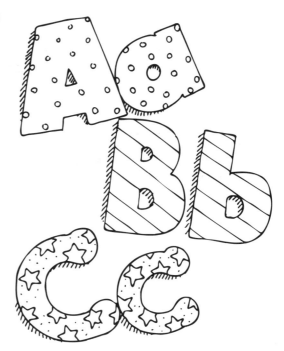

Publishing

Give a piece of construction paper to a student, and ask him or her to create a cover for the class book. Use a hole punch and paper fasteners to bind the pages in alphabetical order between the student-made cover and another piece of construction paper. Place the new nonfiction alphabet book in the book corner or school library. It will be a crowd pleaser!

Book title

by _____

Unwrapping a Book © 2006 Creative Teaching Press

Biography

Researching and writing nonfiction to better understand others is an important concept for children to grasp. Children will naturally become more constructive readers and writers if this skill is introduced in the primary grades. For example, an in-depth study of an author allows children to better understand his or her craft and style. Children will be encouraged to see that everyday experiences influence successful people.

Reading Selections

Martin's Big Words: The Life of Dr. Martin Luther King, Jr. by Doreen Rappaport (Hyperion Books for Children)

Abe Lincoln: The Boy Who Loved Books by Kay Winters (Simon & Schuster)

George Washington Carver: The Peanut Wizard by Laura Driscoll (Grosset & Dunlap)

A Weed Is a Flower: The Life of George Washington Carver by Aliki (Aladdin)

Materials

» Biography Research reproducibles (pages 45–46)
» access to the Internet
» a variety of books about famous people
» blank hardcover books (available through mail-order catalogs)
» crayons and permanent markers
» extra school photos (optional)
» watercolor paints
» paintbrushes

Before Writing

Ask children to consider whom they would like to write a biography about. Make copies of the Biography Research reproducibles (pages 45–46). There are many Web sites geared to the reading levels of young children that provide them with interviews of authors and famous people. Teach children basic Internet exploration techniques, and then have them search for the information outlined on the reproducibles.

Writing

Have children use their completed Biography Research reproducibles to draft a biography. When children are editing their papers, encourage them to incorporate text organizers (e.g., an index), vivid vocabulary, captions, and text boxes into their final versions. If children have already created the desert book, they will know what to do. If they have not done that assignment, refer to the Writing section on page 39 for more detailed instructions.

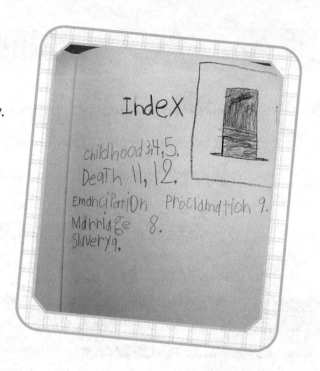

Publishing

Have children add details such as a table of contents, an ISBN code, and an excellence seal to encourage them to take pride in their work. Discuss and review with children the titles of biographies they or their classmates have read. Afterward, children will more easily compose an appropriate title for their piece. Have children use the crayon resist technique (described on page 39) to create a cover for their biography.

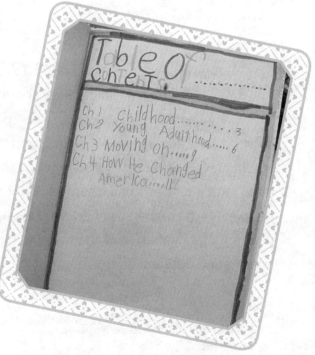

Biography Research

Name: _____

When he/she lived: _____

Died at age: _____

Where he/she lived: _____

_____

Childhood events:

1. _____

_____

2. _____

_____

3. _____

_____

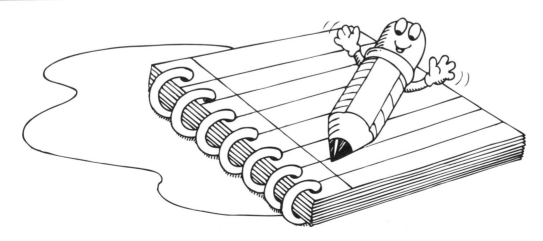

Researcher's Name _____

Biography Research

Adulthood events:

1. _____

_____

2. _____

_____

3. _____

_____

Most important contribution:

_____

_____

_____

_____

Any other information:

_____

_____

_____

Unwrapping a Book © 2006 Creative Teaching Press

Field Guide to Animals

Field guides are excellent tools to integrate science and language arts curriculum. Trying to pack many different lessons into a day (each having its own objective) can be overwhelming to children and teachers alike. Why not concentrate the objectives into one rich and meaningful activity? For example, if your students are studying different animals in science, have them write a field guide after they have done some research on the subject. This ensures that children are reading and comprehending, organizing information, and learning subject matter at the same time.

Reading Selections	Materials
Alaska's Three Bears by Shelley Gill (Paws IV) *The Emperor's Egg* by Martin Jenkins (Candlewick Press) *Javelinas* by Lola M. Schaefer (Heinemann)	» animal research reproducible (page 49) » a selection of nonfiction about animals » 11" x 17" (28 x 43 cm) paper » 12" x 18" (30.5 x 46 cm) construction paper » crayons and markers » hole punch » paper fasteners

Provide the class with a selection of nonfiction about animals. Have the children work in pairs or individually to read the books. Ask pairs of children to choose an animal they want to research, and have them work together to take notes on that subject. Tell them to include the following information in their notes: a description of the animal, what it eats, how it moves, how it protects itself, its life cycle, and its habitat. Also ask children to include the title, the author's name, and the publication date of the resource they are using.

Writing

Enlarge and copy the animal research reproducible (page 49) on 11" x 17" (28 x 43 cm) paper, and give one to each child. Have children transfer their recorded information to their reproducible. If you prefer, have children skip the note-taking stage, and simply ask them to record their findings directly on the reproducible.

Each section of the research reproducible reflects important science concepts for primary grade students. Encourage children to reread the information after they write it, and ask them to use crayons and markers to illustrate the animal, its life cycle, and its habitat with care. Early research skills are further enhanced when children record the title, author, and publication dates of their resources. Writing bibliographies will be made easier in the upper grades when children are familiar with recording their resources.

Publishing

Ask the children to help you organize the pages of the "Classroom Field Guide to Animals" according to similarities and differences among the researched animals. This will lead children to classify animal types. For instance, place the pages about mammals in one section and discuss how birds, reptiles, amphibians, fish, and insects each belong in their own sections. After the pages are assembled, use the construction paper, hole punch, and paper fasteners to bind the pages into book form. Write the title *Classroom Field Guide to Animals* on the cover, and choose a child to illustrate it. Display the classroom book in the reading corner.

Researcher: _____

_____
(type of animal)

What does the animal look like?
_____

What does the animal eat?
_____

How does the animal get around?
_____

How does the animal protect itself?
_____

Life Cycle

_____

_____

_____

_____

_____

Habitat or Region

_____

Resources

Title: _____

Author: _____

Publication date: _____

How-to Book

Writing step-by-step directions can be a difficult task for young children, but how-to books make it fun. Publishing their own how-to books requires children to notice details and look at their writing objectively in order to decide whether or not the directions are clear. Children who love to make things will love publishing these books!

Reading Selections	Materials
Lights! Camera! Action! How a Movie Is Made by Gail Gibbons (Crowell) ***Models*** by Helen Bliss (Crabtree) ***Wild West Days: Discover the Past with Fun Projects, Games, Activities, and Recipes*** by David C. King (Wiley)	» chart paper » blank hardcover books » crayons or markers » supplies to test activity directions

Read a how-to book to the class. On chart paper, make a list of the steps that were detailed in the reading. Ask the children to think about something they can make. Responses may vary from making peanut butter and jelly sandwiches to making a paper airplane. For example, a child may choose to describe how to make a "Cinderella" carriage from a pumpkin and Lego Dacta blocks. Advise children to write about something that they are familiar with or something that has steps that can be tested easily.

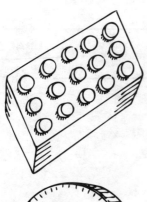

Writing

Ask children to write down the steps it will take to make the object of their choice. Have them trade papers with a neighbor. Tell children to read and follow their classmates' directions to see if the steps are clear. Try to provide as many supplies as possible so that their ideas can be tested. Encourage the "tester" to give constructive feedback to the writer. Have children edit their directions as needed—until the drafted version of the directions has been deemed easy to follow.

Publishing

These books are similar in construction to the desert books described on page 39. Remind children to include a page dedicated to honoring the author, an appealing and informative cover, and any other features they think will give their book a "professional" look.

Display the how-to books alongside the subject items that children have constructed. These make attractive displays for showcases, libraries, classroom reading corners, or a special exhibit for open house night or parent conference week.

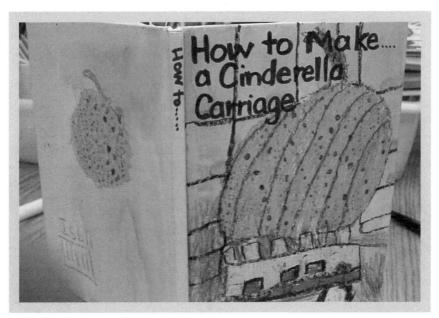

Photo Journal

Showing children how to make a photo journal helps you foster children's creativity while they are learning a new skill. When children use captions to describe their own photos, they are learning to write to inform an audience and use common nonfiction features at the same time. Children will love to practice their new photography skills while they confirm that reading and writing can be fun!

Reading Selections	Materials
Cameras by Chris Oxlade (Gareth Stevens Publishing) **Click! A Book about Cameras and Taking Pictures** by Gail Gibbons (Little, Brown and Company) **What a Job!** by Becky Gold (Chelsea Clubhouse)	» Photo-Journal Planning Sheet (page 54) » old cameras (for labeling) » digital or disposable cameras » sticky notes » blank hardcover books » crayons and markers » watercolor paints » paintbrushes

Read your selection to the class. If possible, have old or broken cameras available for the children to explore. Use a bright color marker to write names of camera parts on sticky notes to make labels for the parts of a camera. This will not only promote rich discussions, but will familiarize the children with new vocabulary. Brainstorm with children a list of subjects for a photo journal (e.g., P. E. class, trees, the class's pet guinea pig).

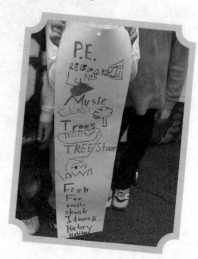

Divide the class into small groups or pairs of children, and ask them to choose their subject from the brainstormed list. Help children carefully plan the photos they wish to take for their book. This planning step will prevent "wasted" snapshots. Make copies of the Photo-Journal Planning Sheet (page 54), and give one to each child (if children are working in pairs, you may want to give them one or two extra copies). Use it to conference with the group before pictures are actually taken. Ask children to decide what information is important to reveal about their subject. Encourage them to imagine what photos will best convey that information. For example, if children are doing a photo journal about nature and want to tell how to discover the age of a tree, they will want to include a picture of the rings in a tree stump. Have one child draw a picture of the rings in a tree stump on his or her planning sheet. (Each child's planning page will show different pictures that the group wishes to include in its photo journal.) Then ask children to write captions to go with the sketches on their planning sheet. The captions should be informative and relevant to the image.

Schools often have digital cameras available for teacher and student use. If this is not the case at your school, purchase inexpensive disposable cameras from a discount store. Demonstrate the use of the camera for children, and then have them take their planned photographs.

Once the photos have been printed, ask the groups to spread out their photos and decide which ones they will use. Encourage children to evaluate pictures for clarity, and let them know that some photos may be cropped (trimmed) if necessary.

When children have prepared their photos and edited their captions, ask them to arrange the photos in their hardcover book and transfer the information from the planning sheet to the book. Have children finish their photo journal in much the same way as the desert book (see page 39). The technique of crayon resist can be used to create the cover. A seal of excellence adds a professional touch to the photo journal and is guaranteed to create a sense of pride in children.

Name _____

Photo-Journal Planning Sheet

sketch of photo   caption

_____

_____

_____

_____

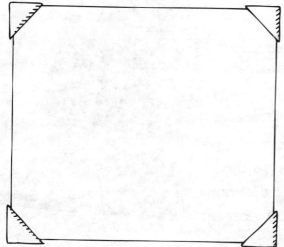

_____

_____

_____

_____

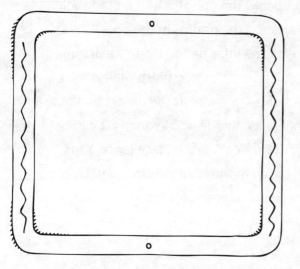

_____

_____

_____

_____

Time Line Book

Throughout their school years, children are asked to use time lines to obtain information. Introducing time lines in the primary grades helps develop good reading habits and gives children yet another way to express information in writing. To teach this topic, choose a reading selection that best suits your students' interests.

Reading Selections	Materials
Chicks & Chickens by Gail Gibbons (Holiday House) ***Claude Monet*** by John Malam (Carolrhoda Books) ***Life Cycle of a Chicken*** by Angela Royston (Heinemann) ***Look to the North: A Wolf Pup Diary*** by Jean Craighead George (HarperCollins)	» chart paper » blank and lined index cards » glue » crayons and markers » spiral-bound black construction paper or side-grip report covers

Before Writing

Read your selection to the class. Discuss the time lines contained in the book. Ask children to retell the information they learned. Write their responses in a time line format on chart paper.

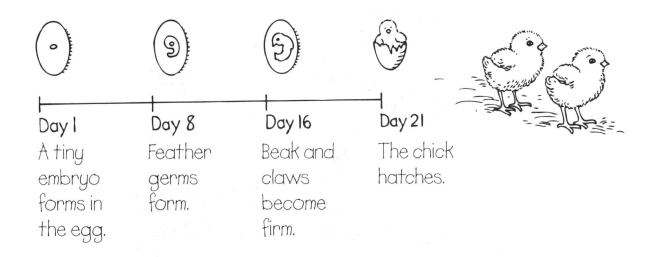

Day 1
A tiny embryo forms in the egg.

Day 8
Feather germs form.

Day 16
Beak and claws become firm.

Day 21
The chick hatches.

Writing

Have children describe the events in chronological order on index cards. Give each child several lined and several blank index cards. Have children write each event on one lined index card (e.g., they may describe the first stage of a chick's life). Then have them illustrate a picture to go with each event on the blank index card. Encourage children to write a rough draft of each stage of development on notebook paper and edit it before copying the information onto the index card.

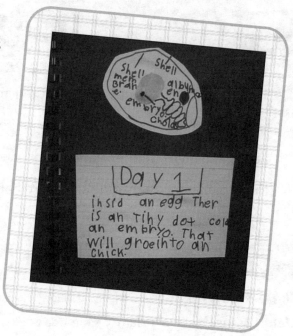

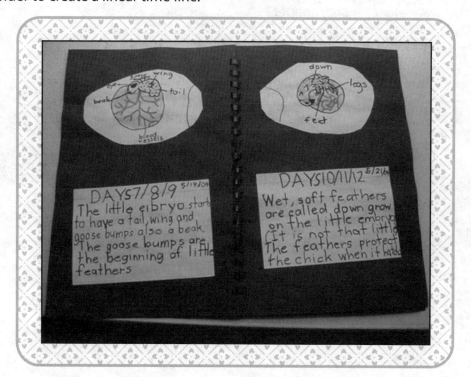

Publishing

Ask children to glue the index cards onto the construction paper. Each page should depict one event in the subject's life. Have children give their time line an appropriate title, and ask them to create a cover page for it. If you are using side-grip report covers, the construction pages will be loose. Help children arrange the pages in order before binding them in their report covers. Show children how to remove the pages from their folder to create a linear time line.

Writing Periodicals

Reporting news that affects their lives comes naturally to children. They are always eager to share and discuss recent events. Whether the news is about the school's field day, a current event from the local news, or something special that happened at home (e.g., the birth of a new sibling), children are born storytellers. Make the most of their enthusiasm by helping them record the information they find noteworthy in a format they can take pride in. Children will love contributing to and reading from a class newspaper and a separate sports magazine.

Classroom Newspaper

Children will read the newspaper! It's guaranteed when the classroom becomes the newsroom. Children transform into researchers, writers, editors, advertisers, illustrators, cartoonists, and publishers. Meaningful writing is created when children share news that is real to them with an audience that cares—their classmates!

Reading Selections

Deadline! From News to Newspaper by Gail Gibbons (HarperCollins)

The Furry News: How to Make a Newspaper by Loreen Leedy (Holiday House)

Extra! Extra! The Who, What, Where, When and Why of Newspapers by Linda Granfield (Orchard Books)

Materials

Preparation

» bookshelf
» black butcher paper
» construction paper
» crayons and markers
» tape
» newspapers and magazines

Materials

Publication

» Planning reproducibles (pages 65–69)
» chart paper
» 24" x 18" (61 x 46 cm) newsprint
» 11" x 17" (28 x 43 cm) paper
» newspapers and magazines
» computer or word processor
» tape recorders
» digital camera

Set up the classroom to resemble a newsroom. Make a special newsstand from an old bookshelf or other structure. Cover it with black butcher paper, and tape signs on it that get people's attention (e.g., *Extra, Extra! Read all about it!*). Read newspapers and news magazines geared to children (e.g., *The Kids' Post*, *Time for Kids*), and place them at the newsstand. Read your selection to the class.

Publication

Hold a publication meeting. Identify the different sections you would like to include in your newspaper (e.g., Travel, Arts, Sports). Write the names of the departments on chart paper. Ask the children to write their names under the section or sections for which they would like to write. Meet with small department groups and model completion of the appropriate research sheets (page 65–69). For example, meet with the children who want to write for the Sports section and help them fill out the Planning a Sports Article reproducible (page 67) using an article taken from one of the papers at your newsstand. See pages 60–64 for newspaper section ideas.

Encourage children to research any of their topics using the real papers and magazines at the newsstand. Provide children with library access, closely supervised access to the Internet, and tape recorders for interviews. Remind children that some articles may need illustrations to accompany them. Children may also require the use of a digital camera to report on a current event, such as the arrival of a new principal.

As the editor-in-chief, compile the articles and arrange them in sections. Type them on the computer, and print the pages on large paper. Ask children to help you use a glue stick to mount the articles on newsprint. You may wish to assemble multiple newspapers for the classroom, the library, and the office.

Front Page

Discuss current events from outside the school with children. Have them choose topics that interest them or topics that were in the headlines of your local newspaper. Ask children who are interested to write a front-page article based on that information.

Masthead

Give your paper an authentic look by including a masthead on the second page. The masthead is comprised of the names of the children, the address of the school, the publisher, the editor, and the founding date. Children will enjoy opening the paper and finding their own names.

Local News

"Local" in this case means within the classroom or school. Have the children compose articles about class news, including field trips, assemblies, and interviews with students and teachers. They may also choose to write about the weather and interesting information they learn during the year.

Editorial and Letters to the Editor

The editor-in-chief often writes the editorial in daily papers, so the editor-in-chief of the classroom paper (the teacher) writes this important article. Give children the opportunity to write their opinion on a current issue in the form of a letter to the editor.

Sports

Many children will be eager to write articles for the sports section. Encourage children to write about the after-school sports they play. Or have them write about current sports events or their favorite sports heroes/teams.

Advice Column

Choose a child to write a "Dear Abby" column. Give the column another name if you wish. For example, if a child named MacKenzie is going to write this section, you may choose to name the column "Dear Mac." Remind children that all letters to "Abby" must involve some kind of a problem, and they must be signed with a pseudonym.

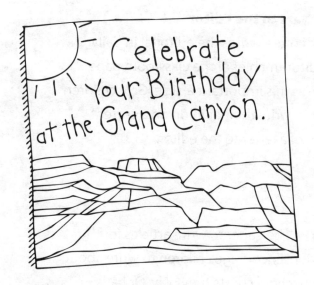

Celebrate Your Birthday at the Grand Canyon.

Travel

The travel section of your newspaper can include articles about places ranging from Arizona to Iran—anywhere the children have traveled. This section offers an opportunity to highlight the cultural diversity now found in our classrooms. It is an excellent launching pad for learning about different states, provinces, and countries. Encourage children to bring in artifacts (e.g., postcards, books, photos) to be used as resources to research the articles.

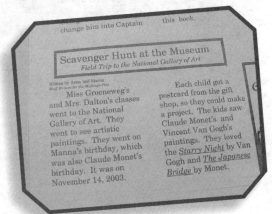

change him into Captain   this book.

Scavenger Hunt at the Museum
Field Trip to the National Gallery of Art

Written by Anna and Manna
Staff Writers for the MyImage Post

Miss Groeneweg's and Mrs. Dalton's classes went to the National Gallery of Art. They went to see artistic paintings. They went on Manna's birthday, which was also Claude Monet's birthday. It was on November 14, 2003.

Each child got a postcard from the gift shop, so they could make a project. The kids saw Claude Monet's and Vincent Van Gogh's paintings. They loved the *Starry Night* by Van Gogh and *The Japanese Bridge* by Monet.

Arts

Like every good newspaper that has an Arts section, highlight local theater, movie, and book reviews. It is an excellent arena to showcase favorite books rather than simply writing a traditional book report.

Food

Have children become food critics. Encourage them to research their articles for the food section by reading a variety of international and other cookbooks checked out from the school library. The subject of these articles may range from chocolate to Japanese rice. Even some favorite family recipes can be highlighted in these articles.

CHOCOLATE Dessert

Style

The style section includes articles on fashion and shopping. It also contains advertisements created by the children. Articles such as "Fashions: Eid Style" and "Ponchos: The Newest Fashion Trend" can be featured in this section.

Obituaries

Although this is a very sad section of the newspaper, it can also be very cathartic for some children

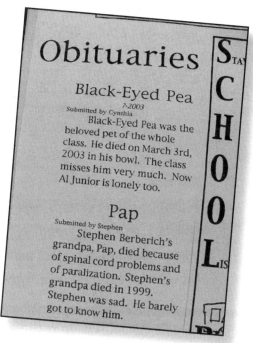

who have had to cope with deaths of grandparents or pets. Discuss with children whether or not they want to include an obituary section.

Announcements

Give your class the opportunity to celebrate happy events in an Announcements section. Invite children to share exciting news in this section of the newspaper. For instance, children may write about the birth of a new sibling or a marriage in the family.

Classifieds

"Help Wanted" and "Services Available" are common headings for various classified ads. Ask the children if they wish to offer free services in areas ranging from spelling assistance to help in drawing pictures. Challenge them to think of services they would be willing to offer anyone in the school building at no cost. Give only the classroom number and the classroom telephone number for contacting these children for their services. You may also wish to advertise classroom jobs, such as messengers, leaders, and table captains in the "Help Wanted" section.

Comics

Although this is an especially challenging task, children will love writing and reading this section. Give each cartoonist a blank strip of paper on which to sketch out his or her idea. Once three other children have deemed the cartoon funny and easy to understand, tell the writer to copy a final version with a thin black felt-tip marker.

Crossword Puzzle

Make a crossword puzzle that contains vocabulary words and concepts taught within the school year. Children will be eager to solve these puzzles and even more enthusiastic to write their own.

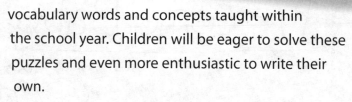

Planning a Featured Story

Who? _____

_____

What? _____

_____

Where? _____

_____

When? _____

_____

How? _____

_____

Other comments: _____

_____

_____

Planning a Newspaper Article

Title: _____

Lead Sentence: _____

_____

Facts:

1. _____

_____

2. _____

_____

3. _____

_____

4. _____

_____

5. _____

_____

End: _____

_____

Unwrapping a Book © 2006 Creative Teaching Press

Planning a Sports Article

Sport: _____

Teams: _____

Score: _____

_____

When and where? _____

_____

Key players: _____

_____

Other comments: _____

_____

_____

_____

_____

_____

Name _____

Planning a Letter to the Editor

What is the issue? _____

_____

What side are you on? _____

_____

What do you think should be done about the issue? _____

_____

_____

_____

_____

Give three reasons to support your point of view. _____

_____

_____

_____

_____

_____

Unwrapping a Book © 2006 Creative Teaching Press

Name _____

Planning a Review

Title of play, film, or book: _____

_____

Who are the characters? _____

_____

_____

Who are the actors or authors? _____

_____

_____

What did you think about the play/movie/book? _____

_____

_____

Give three opinions. _____

_____

_____

_____

Sports for Kids Magazine

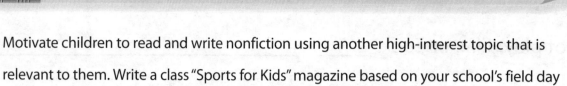

Motivate children to read and write nonfiction using another high-interest topic that is relevant to them. Write a class "Sports for Kids" magazine based on your school's field day or other sports event. Choose a reading selection that best suits your students' interests.

Reading Selections	Materials
Soccer around the World by Dale E. Howard (Children's Press) ***I Can Be a Baseball Player*** by Carol Greene (Children's Press) ***Going to My Gymnastics Class*** by Susan Kuklin (Bradbury Press)	» cameras » glue » construction paper or card stock

Before Writing

Schedule this project around field day. Ask parent volunteers to take digital photos of all the children in your class competing in field day. You are sure to get many action shots! Set up a center with sports magazines and books, and read your selection to the class.

Each child will love to write about his or her favorite sport. Have children choose a sport and write an article on what they have learned about that sport. Alternatively, ask children to write articles on their favorite field day stations. Encourage the "reporters" to interview field day participants and use their classmates' quotes in the articles.

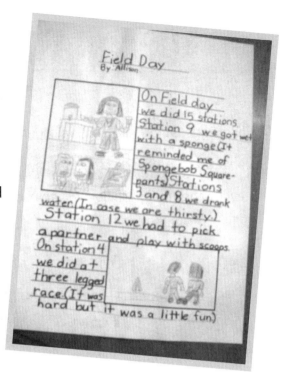

Collect the action snapshots taken by the parent volunteers. Have children write captions and articles for these pictures. The pictures and captions can accompany existing articles or be enlarged for use on separate pages.

Ask children to help you arrange the photos, captions, and articles in an attractive and logical order. Choose one of the photographs to make the cover. If possible, enlarge the photo, and print it in color with the title *Sports for Kids*. Then glue it onto construction paper or card stock. Ask children to help you write smaller captions (teasers) that relate to the contents of the magazine to include on its cover. Smaller snapshots can also be placed on the cover to give the magazine an authentic look. Laminate the cover for durability.

Special Forms of Nonfiction

Encourage children to explore other types of nonfiction writing. Brochures/pamphlets and personal correspondence are two very different forms of writing, but children need help developing their proficiency with each one. Compare and contrast the characteristics of these two genres with children to reinforce how the author's purpose determines the form of writing he or she chooses.

Brochures and Pamphlets

Have your class create brochures and pamphlets about recycling to convey that nonfiction texts have the power to persuade and inform consumers. These recycling brochures can be displayed in the office, staff lounge, or near trash cans in the school cafeteria. Writing for a known audience gives even more meaningful purpose to children's writing.

Reading Selections	Materials
Recycle! by Gail Gibbons (Little, Brown and Company) *Where Does the Garbage Go?* by Paul Showers (HarperCollins) *The Great Trash Bash* by Loreen Leedy (Holiday House) *Recycling* by Rhonda Lucas Donald (Children's Press)	» chart paper » 9" x 12" (23 x 30.5 cm) construction paper » stapler » crayons and markers

Read your selection to the class. Ask children to share their family's recycling plans. Review information from the book, and write it on chart paper. Then, make a class graph depicting the items that each family recycles. Discuss the results. You may also wish to develop a recycling plan as a class to facilitate interest in the subject.

Writing

Tell children to choose what material (e.g., glass or metal) their brochure will focus on recycling. Encourage them to use the chart, the graph, or knowledge gleaned from other sources to decide what information they want to include in their recycling brochure. Have children draft and edit their sentences on notebook paper. Ask the children to choose a fact they find interesting to reserve for printing on the back of their brochure.

Publishing

Have children create a flip book–style brochure. Tell them to lay two sheets of construction paper lengthwise in front of them. Have children arrange the papers so that the bottom page peaks out 1 inch (2.5 cm) from behind the other. Help children fold the top part of the pages over so that a 1-inch margin is created between each tier. Ask children to staple the papers at the top. Tell children to transfer the information from their notebook paper to the brochure, and have them illustrate the facts. Encourage children to give their brochure a title, and ask them to illustrate the cover attractively. Display the finished products in the school office, cafeteria, or staff lounge.

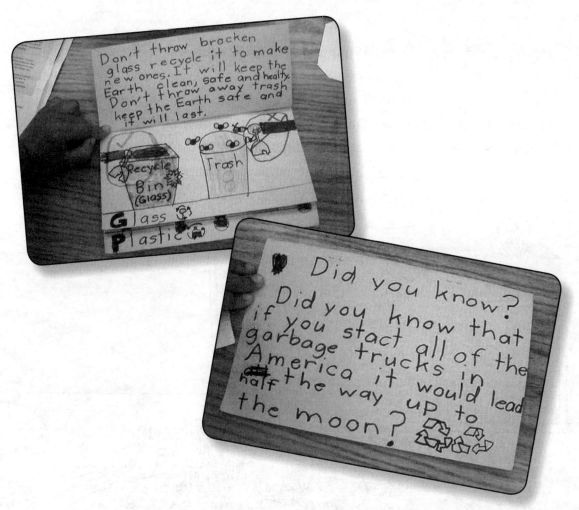

Cards and Letters

Personal correspondence helps us maintain and build relationships. Children love to make cards for each other! Why not practice this form of nonfiction writing by sending cards and letters to a friend or favorite author? When the classroom becomes the post office, children delight in writing cards and letters. Establish a writing center with special types of paper, envelopes, pens, and markers. This writing area will be a hit with your students!

Reading Selections

At the Post Office by Carol Greene (Child's World)

Here Comes the Mail by Gloria Skurzynski (Bradbury Press)

Mail Carriers by Dee Ready (Bridgestone Books)

The Post Office Book: Mail and How It Moves by Gail Gibbons (HarperTrophy)

Materials

» real mailbox or box decorated to look like a mailbox (optional: Mailbox from Creative Teaching Press, CTP 5988)
» colored paper (ruled and plain)
» index cards
» boxed cards
» envelopes
» notepads
» shopping-list pads
» colored pencils
» crayons and markers

Before Writing

Read *The Post Office Book: Mail and How It Moves* with the class. Turn the classroom into a post office! Make a mailbox or purchase an inexpensive one from your local hardware store. Establish a special area for creating cards and letters. Place a variety of writing materials at a writing center. If you can, schedule a field trip to the post office to energize this project. Or perhaps invite someone who works at the post office to come and speak to your class.

Ask children to think of all the different reasons there are for writing letters (e.g., to keep in touch, to express sympathy, to ask for information). Have children think about whom they would like to write a letter to.

 **Writing**

Ask children to keep in mind the purpose of the card or letter as they write. Encourage children to decorate their cards or letters appropriately (e.g., a sympathy card will show a different picture than a congratulatory card). Practice with children how to address mail after they enclose their letters in envelopes.

Publishing

Use the mailbox for classroom deliveries. Appoint a "postmaster" and "letter carriers" to deliver the mail. Recipients of this mail will enjoy reading the notes. You can also send letters to favorite authors through their publishers. Who knows, the children may even get a letter from the author in return!

Board Games and More

Children will love to share what they have learned from nonfiction books by making their own board games! These board games become interactive activities that are guaranteed to help children learn facts while they're having fun. All nonfiction books can be used for this project. If you wish, tailor the book choices to those that match standards-based objectives in your district.

Bring in a variety of board games in order for children to become familiar with the "parts" of these games. Have them play different types of board games until they are familiar with different sets of rules and styles of play (e.g., Chutes and Ladders and Sorry!).

Have children work on their project at home. Encourage them to involve their entire family in their learning. Send home the Make a Board Game reproducible (page 78) for homework for parents' and children's reference.

You will see children create a variety of games on a variety of subjects. Set aside a special day to "celebrate" nonfiction learning by playing the games. This is a marvelous way of reviewing units or ending a school year. If the children are willing to part with their games, keep a few for rainy days in the next school year.

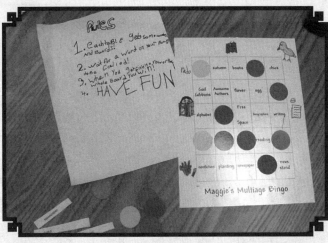

Name _____

Make a Board Game

Think of what you've learned from nonfiction books. Choose one topic to be the theme of your board game.

Your board game should have the following parts:
- Directions
- A board
- All of the pieces ("men", dice, spinner, counters, etc.)
- A box or container that shows what your game is about and will make others want to play it

You will have two weeks to complete this homework assignment. Work on the project a little bit each day so that you won't have too much to do at the end.

Be creative! Work neatly! Enjoy your project!

Due date: _____

We will play our games on _____.

Ideas Using Nonfiction

Reading Response Log—Give children a Reading Response Log (page 80) to complete after they have read a nonfiction selection.

Book Talks—Have children choose their favorite nonfiction books to present to the class. You may wish to make the experience more game-like by asking children to pretend they are on a morning news show at school.

Story Quilts—After reading several nonfiction selections, have children either draw pictures from the books or write facts about the stories on quilt squares. Provide children with 9" (23 cm) squares of white construction paper and crayons or markers. When children are finished decorating their squares, help them arrange the "quilt squares" on a piece of brightly colored butcher paper, and hang the "quilt" in the hallway outside your room. Place a title above the quilt, such as *Quilts Can Tell a Story . . .*

Overlays—You may wish to add overlays to the Features of Nonfiction Text section of this resource. Overlays are excellent tools to view internal and external details of objects (e.g., overlays can show life within a saguaro cactus). To make overlays, use a transparency sheet and permanent markers. Place the transparency over the illustration, and tape it into place. These overlays add interest for authors as well as readers.

Name _____

Reading Response Log

Read a nonfiction book, and answer the following questions.

Title: _____

Author: _____

Write one fact you already knew about the subject of the book: _____

_____

_____

Write two facts you learned from the book:

1. _____

_____

2. _____

_____

What else would you like to learn about this subject?

_____

_____

_____

On another sheet of paper, draw a picture of something in the book that interested you. Don't forget to give it a caption!